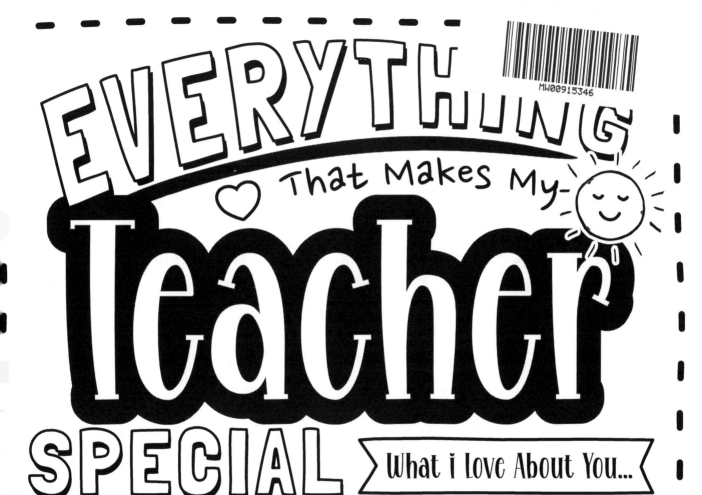

# EVERYTHING

♡ That Makes My

# Teacher

# SPECIAL

What i Love About You...

# ~ contents ~

1. Prompts, Drawing & coloring

2. Letter to my teacher

Written By...

Here's a drawing of my teacher

You are...

_____

(one word to describe my teacher)

Thank you for ALWAYS encouraging me to...

_____

My FAVORITE thing about you is...

_____

You've helped me GROW and get better at...

_____

My FAVORITE activity we did this year was...

_____

You're the BEST at making...

SUPER FUN!

THANK YOU
- for helping me -
LEARN
AND SHINE

I LOVE how you make learning FUN by...

_____

You ALSO make every lesson feel...

_____

I will NEVER forget the time you...

_____

I always feel SPECIAL when you...

_____

I appreciate how you always...

_____

when we...

· · · · · · · · · · · · · · · · · · · · · · · · · · · ·

You make me excited to LEARN about...

_____

You're the
# BEST
# TEACHER!

Thank you for helping me...

_____

## Three things you're REALLY good at...

1. _____

2. _____

3. _____

You taught me so much about...

_____

Thank you for never...

_____

You inspire me to...

_____

You make me SMILE when you...

_____

~ Finish the book by writing a short letter to your teacher ~

Dear..._____

(your teachers name)

_____

_____

_____

_____

_____

From _____

49226314R00024